Original title:
The Scarf's Secret Whisper

Copyright © 2025 Creative Arts Management OÜ
All rights reserved.

Author: Atticus Thornton
ISBN HARDBACK: 978-1-80586-204-8
ISBN PAPERBACK: 978-1-80586-676-3

Hidden Voices in the Stitch

A needle dances, oh so sly,
It twirls and spins like a butterfly.
With every loop a secret's shared,
While the buttons giggle, none are spared.

The patterns chatter, threads take flight,
Whispering tales both day and night.
In corners of fabric, jokes are told,
Of stitches that sparkle, and patches bold.

The Loom's Quiet Heart

In the loom where laughter weaves,
Threads of joy hang from the eaves.
Each clack and clatter brings delight,
As yarns get tangled, oh what a sight!

Laces giggle in colors bright,
The fabric chuckles, what a fright!
With every tug, a story spins,
Of playful mishaps and crafty wins.

Beneath the Threads of Daydreams

Underneath where wishes sleep,
The fabric holds the secrets deep.
A fairy's dance, a gnome's disguise,
Stitched with laughter, no surprise.

Each knot a riddle, each seam a game,
Whispering softly, never the same.
From tangle to tangle, stories flow,
In playful whispers that just won't go.

The Fabric of Forgotten Whispers

In folds where silence used to loom,
Echoes wander, filling the room.
A tattered corner, a voice so sly,
Tales of socks lost, oh me, oh my!

The colors giggle, having their fun,
Each thread a whisper, one by one.
They speak of treasures, old and rare,
Tucked in the fibers, beyond compare.

Hushed Tones Underneath

In a drawer where dust bunnies dwell,
A scarf tells tales no one can quell.
It murmurs stories of flirty nights,
Of tangled mistakes and playful fights.

A whisper of colors, a riotous cheer,
A knit of mishaps, both far and near.
With each twist and turn, a giggle's born,
As secrets unwind on a soft, warm morn.

Fluttering Shadows of Tartan

In checkered hues, it dances around,
Flaunting its secrets without making a sound.
It flutters like gossip on fashion's breeze,
Tickling the edges of corporate tease.

Oh, what a yarn in its fabric hides,
Of silly escapades and hitchhiking rides.
With each flap, it shares a snicker or two,
Making the mundane feel brand new.

A Language of Threads

Stitches and seams speak their own tongue,
Torpedoing boredom, a joy just begun.
They gossip in knots, they chuckle in seams,
Weaving together outlandish dreams.

In shades of bright crimson, a wink, and a nod,
Crafting comedies, oh, so odd!
Each twist in the weave, an inside joke,
An invitation for laughter, a jester's cloak.

Silhouette of a Silent Embrace

Drawn close, tucked in, a curious sight,
A hug from the past, warm and light.
It teases the chill with a playful grin,
As it whispers of folly hidden within.

With a flutter and bounce, it dares to say,
'Who needs a map when you've lost your way?'
In this cozy cocoon, the world seems right,
A shroud of giggles dancing in the night.

Whispered Winds of Wool

In a drawer all bunched and tight,
Lived a yarn that loved to fight.
Spinning tales of mischief grand,
Tickling noses, oh so grand!

Knitting needles rolled their eyes,
As the fibers told their lies.
'Twas a blanket in a brawl,
Woolen wisdom, shared by all.

A pom-pom danced upon the floor,
While the thread sang folklore galore.
The bright colors began to clash,
Oh, the snickers, what a splash!

In a world where stitches scheme,
Every knot hides a silly dream.
So listen close, don't miss the chance,
To hear the yarns in their mad dance!

A Tangle of Stories

A ball of yarn took quite a dive,
Rolling round, it felt alive.
It laughed and gurgled in delight,
Spinning stories day and night.

Two needles winked with wicked glee,
Crafting capers, wild and free.
Threads entwined in silly ways,
Got tangled up, sat in a daze.

One spoke of a cat so sly,
That knitted socks for passersby.
While others shared tales of woe,
Of colorful spills in the snow.

The tales grew thick, with twists and bends,
Crafting memory that never ends.
In every knot, a giggle waits,
A tapestry where nonsense creates!

Veils of Hidden Truths

Under layers soft and fine,
Lie secrets, oh how they shine!
A mismatched pair of socks on rain,
Wonders woven with a grain.

Threads that talk and giggle still,
Whispering secrets, oh what a thrill!
Beneath the folds of cozy knit,
Laughter purrs, never quits.

A wild scarf once flew away,
Chased by kittens in a fray.
Caught up high in a tree of dreams,
Fluffy giggles and fuzzy schemes.

So pull the yarn, let's spin the tale,
Of hidden truths that snicker and sail.
In every stitch, a chuckle hides,
A woolly world where fun abides!

An Echo in the Threads

In a bustling nook, fibers collide,
Whispers echo, laughter's tied.
A crochet hook with a sly little grin,
Spinning yarns where jokes begin.

One thread giggled, 'I'm the best!'
While another said, 'I need a rest!'
As colors clashed in crazy rhyme,
Witty repartee stood the test of time.

Their stories looped in silly knots,
Like a tangle of forgotten thoughts.
From cozy wraps to wild frays,
The threads joined forces to create plays.

So unravel the tales, let them find the light,
Every stitch holds a giggle, a delight.
In the chaos, joy transcends,
Echoing laughter that never ends!

Threads of Soft Confession

In a drawer, it lays in wait,
Tales to tell, it can't be late.
A polka dot, a stripe or two,
Each stitch is giggling, 'Guess who?'

It flutters bright like a cheeky clown,
Whispers of laughter in a floppy gown.
When wrapped about with such delight,
It dances 'round, a silly sight!

Silken Murmurs in the Breeze

As the wind picks up with flair,
It sings of secrets, oh so rare.
Twirling tales that tickle your ear,
Echoes of mischief, always near.

From a neck it sways, a flirty tease,
With every breeze, it loves to sneeze.
Chasing pigeons, playing tag,
What a sight; it makes me wag!

Hidden Stories Woven Tight

Every knot tied with a cheeky grin,
Hiding the joy where laughter's been.
A yarn of yarn, a joke on loop,
Weaving moments in a quirky group.

It trips up laughter on the floor,
While whispering tales of days before.
Twisted fibers, tales abound,
It knows the juiciest news around!

Whispered Colors of Memory

Bright hues giggle from the rack,
Spilling secrets, never lack.
Daring blues and sunny yellows,
In every fold, lie silly fellows.

Each color primed for a footloose jest,
A mural of mirth, it's simply the best.
Twists and turns through corners wide,
Injecting fun, like a joyful ride!

The Unraveled Voice of Comfort

Worn in a twist of quirky pride,
It tickles the nose, a fuzzy guide.
Each knot holds a giggle, each loop a grin,
Who knew such warmth could cause such spin?

Threaded with laughter, old tales unfold,
A tale of a cat who thought it was bold.
It danced on the chair, a woolly delight,
A dramatic retreat in the deep of the night.

Furry whispers bounce all around,
As Buttons the dog sits down, spellbound.
With every tug, the story grows bright,
A mischievous snicker at morning's first light.

Cloaked in Subtle Hues

Colors that clash, a sight so bizarre,
It claims to be chic but comes off as a star.
Yellow with polka dots, green in the breeze,
Fashion faux pas or a comfy tease?

Brimming with joy in every fold,
A rainbow of laughter, a measure of bold.
It hides in the closet, a secretive thing,
Waiting to show how much fun it can bring.

Stitched with a grin, and patterns askew,
Each wear tells a story, an adventure anew.
It speaks in soft shades, makes even gray bright,
A whimsical cloak that feels just right.

Soft Stitches of an Untold Tale

Whispers of warmth with each needle's dance,
A yarn that unfolds in a playful prance.
The threads seem to giggle, with stories to weave,
As it wraps round the shoulders, one can't help but believe.

Winding through time, a fabric of cheer,
Each loop, a secret, a jest drawing near.
It tickles the toes, enchants with delight,
Could a textile laugh, or is that just fright?

In cozy embrace, with a cheeky sneer,
It sings of adventures that draw you near.
So stay wrapped and warm, let joy coexist,
In stitches and giggles, we'll never be missed.

The Enigma of Woven Dreams

Tangled in whims, a puzzle of glee,
It tickles the fancy, like bees to a spree.
With clever designs and riddle-like flair,
It dreams of escapades hiding somewhere.

Threads stretch and yawn, like a cat in the sun,
Its patterns are quirky, yet oh, so much fun.
From cozy cocoon to a wild, erratic spin,
Each twist leads to laughter, a joyous din.

Crafted with chaos, yet charmingly neat,
A scarf so mysterious, you'll dance on your feet.
It whispers in colors, both bright and absurd,
In the realm of fabric, let silliness be heard.

Threads of Dreams Beneath the Surface

In the drawer, a tale unwinds,
Where socks and whimsy intertwine.
One sock speaks of a wild romance,
While the other dreams of a top hat dance.

Beneath the bed, loose threads do spin,
With mischievous frays, they laugh, they grin.
A button's lost on a carnival ride,
While a rogue thread hums of a joyride.

They weave together stories so absurd,
Of chilly nights and a mockingbird.
In fabric whispers, giggles collide,
Each fiber a secret, none can hide.

So if you find a stray yarn today,
Listen close—let it lead you astray.
For stitches hold laughter, pure and light,
In whimsical dreams that dance at night.

A Tapestry of Unseen Emotions

A patchwork quilt, bright and loud,
Sobs and giggles in every crowd.
Underneath the fraying seams,
Lie ticklish tales and silly dreams.

A thread of joy pulls tight in fright,
While sadness tries to find the light.
Laughter echoes, a fabric's cheer,
As buttons pop and vanish near.

The snags of life, all whims and fun,
With kaleidoscope threads sewn, just begun.
At the tail end of each little tear,
A chuckle hides, dancing in the air.

So make a patch, let colors play,
Your heart's own fabric, woven each day.
For in those stitches, in jests and cheer,
Lie emotions wrapped, while we all steer.

Fragments of Time, Stitched Together

A mended hem with a silly patch,
Time's quirks all go with a scratch.
With tic-tac toes and frisky stitches,
Each hairpin turn, full of glitches.

Memories cling like lost fringe,
Unraveled still, they sometimes cringe.
An old zipper hums a forgotten tune,
As ribbons tango beneath the moon.

In pockets deep, strange treasures hide,
Buttons and notes, quite the wild ride.
Lost and found, all jumbled around,
Like mismatched socks in the lost-and-found.

So hold that fabric, cherish each fray,
For time's funny twists guide our play.
In every rip, a story to see,
As fibers waltz, wild and free.

Muffled Whispers of Old Patterns

Old patterns laugh from the attic's gloom,
Each twirl of fabric dispels the doom.
They whisper jokes of bygone days,
Silken chuckles in mysterious ways.

Pillow seams hide giggles and sighs,
Chasing with threads that reach for the skies.
A curtain's fold can toss and tease,
While knobby yarns twist and freeze.

Every stitch holds a playful jest,
Of fashion mishaps and a wardrobe quest.
So if you feel the fabric's sway,
Know it's laughing at you today.

In patterns old and seams unstrung,
Life's funny tunes are always sung.
With whispered tales of yesteryear,
Let every fiber bring you cheer!

The Dance of Fiber and Breath

In my closet, a dance ensues,
Fuzzy threads don their silly shoes.
Spinning, twirling, with knots that squeak,
They giggle softly, this is no technique.

A sock slips left, a mitten trips right,
Jumping and jiving, what a sight!
With every twist, a laugh escapes,
It's the fabric world's wild capes.

Each stitch a secret, each thread a song,
They party on merrily, all night long.
But who will tell them when to cease?
Ah, the fibers dance, never needing peace.

Threads of a Thousand Hopes

Each yarn holds dreams of colors bright,
They twist and tangle, a mystical sight.
Some wish for warmth, a cozy embrace,
While others plot to cover up my face!

Oh, the mischief these threads can weave,
They've got tricks up their sleeves, I believe.
A green hue plans to frolic in spring,
While a gray one just wants to do the bling.

Yet amidst this chaos, laughter we find,
With each little knot, memories entwined.
These threads connect hopes, each one a mess,
Who knew such fun lay in this soft dress?

Hidden Messages in a Loom

In the loom, whispers giggle and play,
Every interaction has its own ballet.
A tangled thread that trips the next,
Speaks in riddles, a loom's own text.

What does the twine want; what does it see?
A pair of socks? Or maybe a bee?
Oh, but each twist brings a grin so wide,
As if the fibers have secrets to hide.

With every shuttle, a laugh is spun,
Crafting a tale, oh what fun!
Each stitch a giggle, each knot a tease,
The loom's a jokester, always keen to please.

The Symphony of Stitches

What a symphony, this needleplay,
Stitches chime in their own ballet.
A tap, a snap, they sing with glee,
Cacophonous joy, who could foresee?

In one sweet fabric, lives a wild choir,
Each thread a note, with laughter to inspire.
The pompoms bounce to a cheery tune,
While yarn balls roll under the moon.

Harmony woven with giggles so bright,
A patchwork of whimsy, pure delight.
And though some stitches may feel quite tight,
They dance on, believing in their might.

Secrets Held Tight by Twists

In a corner of the room, it waits,
Tangled tales in woven fates.
A wink from a string, a giggle from lace,
A vibrant dance in a cozy space.

Whispers of laughter, curling around,
Secret puns in each twist are found.
A knot's a story, the end's a jest,
Wrapped in humor, it's truly the best!

Each fold a chuckle, a secret squish,
Unravel the humor, a fabric wish.
With every tuck, a punchline sighs,
A textile comedy that never lies!

The threads conspire, weaving delight,
Creating mischief in fluffy light.
So let them chatter, let them play,
In their soft embrace, join the fray!

Hushed Conversations of Cloth

In shadows soft where fibers creep,
The murmurs build as we all peep.
A scarf, it chuckles, a hat holds tight,
In stitches woven, a comical plight.

"Oh, did you hear the tale of the seam?"
Threads blush bright at the sudden theme.
With every fold, they gossip with glee,
A patchwork chorus, wild and free!

They whisper of colors that never clash,
And jokes unfold in a gentle flash.
Fabrics gossip beneath the bright lights,
Tickling tales in the softest nights.

The world can wear them, a fashion chat,
Yet only they know where the humor's at.
So lend an ear to the cloth's sweet hum,
And laugh along with the secrets they drum!

Echoes From Beneath a Stitch

Beneath each seam, a chuckle lies,
Hidden giggles in fabric guise.
Each needle's prickle, a funny poke,
Weaving mischief in every cloak.

"Have you heard the news from the cuff?"
Threads giggle low, "It's more than enough!"
A ruffle here and a stitch gone wide,
Fabric friendships that can't abide.

In playful patterns, humor weaves,
Jestful threads that no one believes.
They spin and twist in joyous flight,
Whispering secrets well into the night.

So next time you drape something snug,
Spare a thought for the muted shrug.
For laughter's hidden in every fold,
A tale of fabrics waiting to be told!

Threads That Bind the Past

Old spools chuckle, a vibrant crew,
Stitched together by laughs that grew.
From something simple to a glorious twist,
Their sassy chatter cannot be missed.

"Oh dear, remember that last odd sock?"
In a fit of giggles, they start to mock.
Stitches that crossed, a fabric oddity,
Bring forth laughter in pure unity.

With every weave, they share their quirks,
Patterns that dance as history lurks.
A tangle of tales from long ago,
Threads bind us tightly in giggly flow.

So laugh with them, these fibers bright,
For each little stitch holds laughter's light.
In every hem, a legacy's gleam,
With those tangled threads, we all can dream!

Whispers of Comfort in Fabric

In a drawer it hides, oh so sly,
A fuzzy little creature, oh my!
Telling tales of warmth and cheer,
It tickles my neck, brings laughter near.

Each twist and loop holds a jest,
Knots of giggles at the very best.
A dance of colors, playful and bright,
Turning chilly days into delight.

When it's cold, a jolly surprise,
Laughter blooms, the humor flies.
I swirl it round, my trusty friend,
In this fabric world, joy has no end.

Oh, how it whispers in silly tones,
Of best friends, tea, and ice cream cones.
In every thread, a secret cheeky,
My silly scarf, forever sneaky!

Shadows Caught in Knit

In shadowy corners it loves to creep,
Knitted tales that never sleep.
With every stitch, a ticklish tease,
A playful breeze that aims to please.

Wrapped in fibers, it giggles a tune,
Whirling around like a silvery moon.
Circular motions, a comedy scene,
Who knew yarn could be so obscene?

Every purl a punchline, every knit a grin,
It dances with joy, let the fun begin!
Whispers of whimsy in each little fold,
A hug from the past, though it's kind of bold.

Oh, the mischief it wraps so tight,
Brought my dog to join in the fight.
A joyful ruckus, a knotted delight,
Shadows in the knit, we laugh all night!

Secrets Woven in Color

Colors collide in a vibrant shout,
What secrets are hidden? It's time to find out.
Rainbow threads weave a playful jest,
In this wild fabric, hilarity rests.

A twist of red with a splash of green,
Tales of laughter that once were seen.
Quirky patterns, a design of glee,
A comic strip woven just for me.

Leaping loops and a jolly spin,
Who knew wool could make such a din?
It teases the socks, makes them laugh,
In my drawer, there's a yarny giraffe!

Echoes of joy in each playful strand,
With every loop, I'm in high demand.
With this bright cloak, I twirl about,
Secrets in colors, no doubt it's a rout!

The Warm Embrace of Yarn

When the nights turn chilly, I grab my prize,
A warm embrace that's quite a surprise.
It wraps and swirls, a cocoon of joy,
A fuzzy hug from my favorite toy.

Each stitch a cuddle, all snug and tight,
Crafting a comfort that feels just right.
It jokes with my heart, makes me grin,
As frosty winds swirl outside, let's begin!

With every purl, I hear it shout,
Come dance with me, let go of doubt.
Laughter weaves through this yarny delight,
With flicks and fluffs, we take to flight.

So gather round, for warmth we'll share,
With threads of giggles, we banish despair.
In cozy corners, let cheer take root,
The soft, warm embrace is our sweet hoot!

The Mutable Fabric of Dreams

In the closet sat a weave,
With colors that made you believe.
It laughed as it tangled tight,
And danced in the moon's soft light.

Stitches telling tales of glee,
Of yarns that once were free.
It tickles the toes of fate,
In a fabric that's far from straight.

When folded, it whispers loud,
Like a comedian in a crowd.
Each string a punchline, oh what a joke!
Even shoes desire to revoke!

So when you wear this crafty blend,
Be ready for laughter, my friend.
For every twist, a chuckle waits,
In dreams that never slack their gait.

Threads Binding Time in Silence

In a world where time has spun,
Threads of silence come undone.
They giggle through the hours,
In a fabric that has superpowers.

One stitch will pull a wrinkle tight,
Knots tying giggles in delight.
They tease the clocks, take a nap,
While dust bunnies weave their trap.

Here, the fabric fumbles and slips,
Rich with history, shadowy trips.
Tick-tock, it hums a silly tune,
Laughter bubbling like a cartoon.

So if you find that time feels weird,
It's the fibers that you've revered.
In every stretch, a cheeky jest,
Binding moments, and laughter's best.

Unfurled Secrets of Grace

A ribbon danced in a gentle breeze,
Whispering secrets with utmost ease.
It spun and twirled with a silly flair,
   Making socks jealous of its air.

While garments sighed in pale dismay,
The ribbon frolicked and flew away.
It holds invisible charms, oh so sly,
As buttons giggle and zippers comply.

Each fold reveals a tale of fun,
Of swishy skirts and races run.
With every twirl, it sways a song,
   Inviting all to sing along.

So let it lead you with its grace,
Dancing through life at a breakneck pace.
For secrets unfurled bring joy anew,
   In a world woven with laughter's hue.

The Heartbeat of a Woven Tale

In a closet where chaos takes flight,
A fashionista's dreams jump into the night.
With colors that giggle and fabrics that tease,
They plot a grand heist, just wait, if you please.

But fabric knows secrets, oh what a twist,
A ruffled-out sleeve hides a silly fist.
The buttons all chuckle, the threads intertwine,
They threaten to spill fun, just drink the fine wine!

Oh the garb that collides on laundry day strife,
They've tangled in laughter, it's a dress with a life!
With fraying young edges, they dance in delight,
Telling tales of mischief, beneath the moonlight.

But beware the odd sock, it's regal, you see,
It reigns 'neath the bed like the fabric of spree.
With a wink and a sway, it's a cloth-caper plot,
To rally the material, it's fabric... or not!

Soft Fibers Speak in Silence

Underneath my chair, there's a tale yet to tell,
Of fibers that chuckle as they weave their own spell.
With each little stitch, they conspire and scheme,
Turning even the serious into a whimsical dream.

Beneath the soft linens, a giggle erupts,
As tassels plot mischief, no chance of abrupts.
In the realm of the yarn, all seriousness fades,
It's a party of fabric, a dance through the shades.

Oh, the polka-dot ribbons have stories to share,
Of carefree escapades and moments to spare.
In the quietest corners, they whisper and play,
As fibers united sway softly away.

They giggle and gossip in colors so bright,
As tails of amusement catch laughter's delight.
From patchwork to puns, their joy we must hear,
For in the world of textures, hilarity's near!

Enigmas in the Ebb of Textiles

In the folds of the fabric, a riddle takes shape,
With stitches and seams dreaming of escape.
Why is the plaid feeling silly today?
It's tangled in gossip, and just wants to play!

The stripes crack a joke, and they all come alive,
As patterns debate who's the best to survive.
The corduroy grins, with its ribbed sense of pride,
While the silk starts to shimmy and shimmy aside.

In the quilted domains where stories reside,
The colors join forces, refusing to hide.
With threads that weave laughter, they take a bold stand,
Each snicker a whisper, together they band.

So gather your garments, let's dance in the hall,
For in this world woven, there's laughter for all.
In the fabric of humor, we'll lose all our cares,
And find secret giggles beneath textile layers!

Layers of Untold Narrative

Beneath the warm layers, what stories await?
Each fabric a witness to laugh and create.
With jokes tucked away in the seams of each fold,
The warmth of tradition spins tales to be told.

Oh, the outermost layer thinks it knows all,
Yet underneath bubbles a raucous free-for-all.
The knitters and sewers, they rival on lines,
As they spin yarns together, in funny designs.

The silks whisper softly, with secrets galore,
While cotton chimed in, "Let's open this door!"
Together they beckon, a mischievous crew,
To unravel the humor that's woven right through.

So pull on your layers, come join in the fun,
For every stitch tells us, happiness won.
With each tiny thread holding laughter so bright,
In the fabric of friendship, we twinkle through night!

Soft Hues of Quiet Confessions

In the corner of my room, it lies,
A vibrant tale, in woven ties.
Each fold a giggle, each fringe a grin,
Hiding secrets, where fun begins.

A twist of blue, a dash of red,
It tells of things I never said.
Dances on air when breezes blow,
Whispering stories only it knows.

Upon my neck, it starts to tease,
Tickling chin and dancing with ease.
With every wave, it seems to boast,
Of silly moments I love the most.

So here we laugh, as the world spins,
In soft hues where whimsy wins.
A playful charm wrapped tight and neat,
In mischief's cradle, it's oh so sweet.

Frayed Edges of Memory

Patchwork memories, tangled threads,
Each fray a fable, where laughter spreads.
Snags from adventures, a toe in the door,
A giggle escapes, who could ask for more?

A tangle of fibers, a knot in time,
Wrapped close to the heart, in rhythm and rhyme.
With every pull, a chuckle rises,
In the chaos of colors, life surprises.

Throw it on silly, iridescent flair,
It sways like a dancer, without a care.
Worn slightly askew, it starts to prance,
Inviting the world to join in the dance.

Memories captured in delicate weave,
The knotted laughter we smugly cleave.
As daylight fades, we revel in jest,
Frayed edges, our history, we love the best.

The Language of Yarn

A twist of yarn, a wink in the weave,
Speaks in riddles, the mind can believe.
With giggles it frolics, in stitches it plays,
Each loop a chuckle, in whimsical ways.

Oh, the chatter of colors, they converse with cheer,
Whispering secrets, none will hear.
With purls and with knits, they snugly embrace,
Creating a language of warmth and grace.

As I wrap myself in its playful guise,
It blooms like a flower, lifting me high.
In cozy cocoon, we share a jest,
With yarn as my guide, I find the best.

So gather 'round, as the fibers unwind,
In the laughter of yarn, bliss we will find.
We'll spin a tale full of giggles and glee,
In a world made of threads, just you and me.

Secrets Woven in Threads

A tapestry of whims, where secrets collide,
In threads of cheekiness, joy can't hide.
Every loop a punchline, every drift a joke,
In this fabric of laughter, we gently poke.

Stitches so sly, they wink at the past,
Woven with mischief, cast shadows so vast.
Tales of folly, adventures unraveled,
Entwined in yarn where we often traveled.

A playful knot ties my heart to the show,
Whispers of fun in this textile glow.
Hidden jokes dart like fireflies bright,
In the stitches we share, 'til the fall of night.

So wrap me in giggles and knock on the thread,
For a cloak full of laughter is my heart's bed.
As we stitch and we weave, let merriment spread,
In this quilt of our souls, let joy be fed.

The Warmth of Unspoken Words

In pockets where laughter hides,
A tale of warmth and quirks resides.
Each fiber spins a playful thread,
Unveiling secrets never said.

A knot in time, a stitch of glee,
Whispers tickle, wild and free.
With every fold, a chuckle brews,
A giggle here, a playful muse.

Soft edges tease the nose and cheek,
Hints of laughter, far from meek.
Threads entwined, a dance, a tease,
Footloose tales carried on the breeze.

Each layer wraps a cheeky jest,
Wrapped up tight but never stressed.
The joy we share, a yarn so neat,
In cozy knits, we find our beat.

Patches of Silent Memories

A patchwork quilt of tales combined,
With stitching that speaks of the maligned.
Each patch a peek at days gone by,
Where mishaps twinkle, laughter flies.

A bobble here, a snicker there,
Unraveled moments float in air.
Knots of joy, where mischief calls,
In tangled threads, the humor sprawls.

A tangle here, a weave of yarn,
Whispers giggle like a charm.
Memories snicker, never shy,
In every stitch, a wink or sigh.

Playful patterns, just for show,
Where all the funny secrets flow.
In thread and fiber, tales will brew,
From silly threads, our laughter grew.

Layers of Gentle Whispers

In layers soft, like giggles pressed,
A tapestry of fun expressed.
Whispers twine in playful loops,
A banter shared by laughing troops.

Each row a jest, each stitch a wink,
Tales of naughtiness in the pink.
With every turn, a chuckle flows,
In fabric's hug, the laughter grows.

Gentle nudges from hidden seams,
Echo of the crafter's dreams.
Fingers slip as chuckles rise,
In yarn-drenched joy, we find the prize.

Layers that speak without a sound,
In cozy wraps, hilarity found.
The giggles linger, soft and bright,
In every fold, a shared delight.

Soft Encounters in Knitting

In cozy nooks where laughter weaves,
Soft encounters, make-believe.
A purl of joy, a knit of cheer,
Adventures thrive when friends are near.

With every cast-on, tales emerge,
A playful poke, a crafty surge.
As yarn unwinds, secrets unfold,
In each small stitch, a joke retold.

Two pairs of needles clash and clash,
Amidst the yarn, we share a laugh.
Purls that twist like our witty jokes,
In happy moments, the laughter croaks.

Soft wraps abound, each fiber gleams,
In every loop, a spark of dreams.
So grab your yarn, let humor fly,
In knitting's realm, the world's awry.

Whispering Threads of Time

In a cupboard, so deep and wide,
Lies a fabric creature, full of pride.
It tells of adventures, of a cat on a fence,
And how socks go missing, quite often, hence.

Each twist contains stories of yesterdays,
Like a sock puppet's tales in a whimsical haze.
Laughter erupts with a threadbare grin,
As it recounts the times that socks made a win.

From picnics with ants to a dance with a broom,
This fabric entity fills the room.
With stitches so sly, and patterns so steep,
It wobbles and giggles, a secret to keep.

Each fold a whisper, not quite understood,
In the land of the lost, where the mismatched stood.
A tale of mismatches brought to the floor,
Leaving us laughing and begging for more.

The Untold Tales of Fiber

In a basket, tangled, a party of yarn,
Each thread has a story, each fiber a charm.
They plot and they scheme for a runaway show,
Winking at buttons, 'We're all set to go!'

An old woolly scarf, with a patchwork of dreams,
Tells jokes to the needles, or so it seems.
It claims it's a blanket—officially soft,
Yet here in the corner, it may just loft.

A mitten recites their spooky old tales,
Of toe socks and slippers that wandered the trails.
With snickers and chuckles, they spin their old thread,
Entwining the laughter, as they lie on the bed.

In this kingdom of fibers, a party persists,
A gathering of fabric, who can resist?
Each muffled exchange in this jolly attire,
Is a laugh, a giggle, an unending fire.

Silken Secrets in Shadows

In the twilight, where secrets abide,
Silken whispers dance, full of pride.
A bow of bright colors, a secretive giggle,
As lace unveils tales that make you wiggle.

Frayed edges confide of their daring duels,
Where ribbons once tangled and played all the fools.
They chuckle in unison at the dust bunnies' haste,
Giving them life in their thread-laden taste.

Mismatched napkins plot under the moon,
With plans for a party that starts very soon.
Each fold brings a grin, each crease brings a song,
In the shadows of fabric, where secrets belong.

With shed glitter and twinkling delight,
They share every giggle that lasts through the night.
A tapestry woven of laughter and cheer,
Where silken whispers keep friendships near.

In the Fold of Fabric Dreams

In the fold of a shirt, where mischief will bloom,
Dreams take a ride, as they float on the loom.
Socks share their secrets, worn down to the thread,
About jumping in puddles and how they fled.

With arms wide open, the fabrics align,
Each seam a confession, so utterly fine.
A patch of bright blue, with a wink and a twirl,
Invites all to dance, to laugh, and to swirl.

Button eyes gleam as they spin in delight,
With a jolly good story that lasts through the night.
Each pattern holds laughter, each stitch finds a muse,
In this folky wonderland, there's nothing to lose.

Cotton and flannel collide in a ball,
And they giggle together through each fabric wall.
As yarns intertwine in a jubilant blend,
These fabric dreams weave a smile that won't end.

Stories Caught in the Weave

In threads of laughter, tales unfold,
A piebald yarn, both bright and bold.
A kitten tangles in a ball,
While grandma giggles through it all.

With every twist, a secret shared,
The cat's a thief, she doesn't care.
A scarf that dances in the breeze,
With stories whispered with such ease.

Its colors clash, a playful sight,
It sways and bobs, full of delight.
Among the friends, it holds a place,
Comedic grace, a laughing face.

So when you wrap it 'round your neck,
Expect a twist, or something wrecked.
For life itself is often spun,
In funny ways, that leave us stunned.

Embrace of the Woven Whisper

The threads unite, in dances bright,
A blanket hug, a soft delight.
But watch for pranks, as they entwine,
With tickles 'neath that cozy line.

Each fiber boasts a silly claim,
That knitted tales are never lame.
It whispers jokes that make you grin,
As cozy antics waltz within.

Tangled in warmth, a playful fight,
A chase for naps, all through the night.
In gentle folds, the stories tease,
While snoring loudly with such ease.

And when it falls, take heed, beware,
It might just land upon a chair.
With laughter echoing in soft layers,
This woven hug's the best of players.

The Cloak of Soft Shadows

A cloak of whispers, shades arise,
With tales of mischief in disguise.
It follows you like a playful ghost,
A fabric friend, that loves to boast.

Each fold conceals a funny plot,
In shadows cast, it ties a knot.
A wink from fabric, a curly cue,
The curtain sways, its laughter true.

It flutters free, and off it goes,
A playful spirit, whoosh, it blows!
In shadows deep, the giggles bloom,
Beware the cloak, it loves to zoom.

So wrap it snug, and hold it tight,
Expect it to be quite a sight.
For in its seams, a joke concealed,
A funny charm, forever revealed.

Tapestry of Hidden Longings

In woven patches, dreams entwine,
A patchwork quilt of dear designs.
With every stitch, a giggle sewn,
   A tapestry that's all its own.

Each moment caught in playful thread,
While tiny socks parade, it's said.
Bright polka dots with dashes bold,
This quilt is warm, a sight to hold.

Yet underneath, a cat's tail peeks,
As laughter echoes, sly little squeaks.
With seams that hide a tickle war,
   The funny fabric opens doors.

So snuggle up and join the spree,
   In tales that spin so carelessly.
For in this cloth, we find our cheer,
   A tapestry that draws us near.

Enigmatic Patterns in the Dark

In a closet where shadows play,
A polka dot dances, leading astray.
Unexpected, it giggles at night,
Tickling old sweaters, oh what a sight!

Stripes get jealous, they start to twist,
Claiming they're the ones who can't be missed.
Whispers of plaid in a mischievous dream,
Arguing loudly, or so it would seem!

Fluffy fringes sway left and right,
As laughter spills under the moonlight.
A stitch in time saves a silly laugh,
Who knew fabrics could have such a craft?

When dawn breaks, patterns keep their game,
Trying to figure out who's to blame.
In a world where cotton has a say,
Every thread's secret is just a play!

Whispers and Twists Beneath Fabric

Beneath the layers, secrets take flight,
A vibrant swirl claims to be polite.
With every fold, a giggle escapes,
Daring the buttons to join in the shapes!

Lace tells stories of lost, silly days,
While denim just chuckles in rugged ways.
Oh, the tales they weave in a rusty old chest,
Each whisper a jest, let's see who's the best!

Ribbons debate on whose knot is divine,
My bow is prettier — no, mine's truly fine!
Silk softly snickers, feeling quite grand,
Provoking the cotton to take a stand!

When the sun sets and shadows begin,
Under the moon, the fabrics spin.
In the kingdom of threads, all laughter is free,
Where every fold shouts, "Come dance with me!"

Threads of Silken Secrets

In a basket where chaos reigns supreme,
Threads plot mischief, weaving a dream.
Silk and wool trade playful barbs,
Crafting a tale that's full of carbs!

Yarns lie tangled in a funny twine,
Whispering secrets about red wine!
Innocent cotton just rolls its eyes,
While knitters giggle, sharing surprise.

Spools start spinning like dancers at dawn,
Each step a twirl, till the last one's gone.
Hats are all snickering, ready for fun,
Creating a ruckus where none had begun!

With each little twist, they gossip away,
Waiting for moments to burst out and play.
Beneath all the laughter, a secret does dwell,
In the land of the fabrics, all is quite well!

Murmurs in the Fabric

In the folds of everyday wear,
Fabrics share giggles with casual flair.
A whispers of velvet, oh what a tease,
Chasing the linen with the greatest of ease!

Cotton gets cheeky, rolls on the floor,
"Who is the softest? I won this war!"
Denim just chuckles, rugged and tough,
"I wear the battles — I'm made of rough stuff!"

In shadows they play, with puns that ignite,
Stitch by stitch, growing more light!
Every patch has a tale, every seam a jest,
Making mischief, oh, they're the best!

As evenings draw in with stars shining bright,
Threads share their laughter, their secrets of light.
In the quiet of night, they twirl and they tease,
Fabric lives boldly, if you just let it please!

Patterns of Forgotten Echoes

In a drawer, old stories hide,
A tangled mess, not dignified.
They dance with dust, a comical show,
Whispering tales of long ago.

A floral print, a polka dot,
These old friends, they've got a lot!
They laugh at spills and epic falls,
And fashion faux pas from shopping malls.

Each thread a memory, quite absurd,
Of times we tripped, and sadly blurred.
They giggle at how we were dressed,
Echoes of laughter, never repressed.

In a swirl of colors, they conspire,
To remind us of days that never tire.
With a wink and a nudge, they slyly say,
"Wear us again, it's a silly play!"

Woven Echoes of Lost Days

In the closet, they plot and scheme,
Bringing back memories, like a dream.
With every fold, a chuckle rings,
Of mismatched socks and silly flings.

The patterned chaos, a bright delight,
Faded colors, yet spirits bright.
Frayed edges whisper tales of yore,
Of adventures that they can't ignore.

They've seen it all, through thick and thin,
Splashing through puddles, with goofy grins.
With every thread, a punchline waits,
In the fabric of fate, where laughter creates.

Faded hues tell of dances bold,
Outrageous moves, or so we're told.
These woven echoes, in joyous cheer,
Remind us of all we hold dear.

The Silent Saga of Softness

In cozy corners, they softly lay,
Muffled giggles from yesterday.
Each fold a giggle, each crease a laugh,
In the tales they weave, one can't do half.

A swoosh of fabric, a playful tease,
As if they plot to catch a breeze.
They hint at secrets, silly and bright,
Beneath the daylight, out of sight.

With snickers hiding in every seam,
They tell of childhoods and silly dreams.
In an embrace, they hold their cheer,
Whispering softly, "We've been right here!"

They cuddle close, their warmth a jest,
In their silent saga, we're all blessed.
Forever soft, they tickle the heart,
A tapestry woven with laughter as art.

Cascading Threads of Intimacy

From the hook, they tumble down,
Laughing as they hit the ground.
A riot of colors, a carefree fling,
Entangled giggles, oh what joy they bring!

Each twist and turn tells a tale,
Of clumsy dances, where we pale.
Fraying edges, yet never sad,
A reminder of all the fun we had.

They flutter like butterflies, bold and bright,
In the breeze of memories, pure delight.
Whispering softly through every fold,
Stories of warmth, forever told.

A mishmash of patterns, a cozy bond,
In their playful chaos, we respond.
Threads of intimacy, oh what a gift,
In every loop, our spirits lift.

Veils of Warmth and Mystery

A scarf so bright, it steals the show,
Knits tales of joy, wrapped high and low.
It dances in breezes, a cheeky sprite,
Whispering secrets, oh what delight!

In chilly winds, it shimmies and sways,
A silly creature, on windy days.
It tickles the chin, makes noses twitch,
In a game of warmth, it's quite the witch!

The colors chime like a jolly song,
Hiding surprises, where they belong.
A sly little gnome, stitched with zest,
In the land of neckwear, it's truly the best!

So if you see it lounging around,
Know it's plotting mischief with each round!
With every twist, it jests and beams,
A fabric prankster, living in dreams.

Echoes in Fabric

Fabric soft as a kitten's purr,
With patterns that twist and often stir.
Socks may feel lonely without a mate,
But watch this scarf dance—it's kinda great!

Whispers of laughter in every thread,
It chit-chats with hats—what's that you said?
A faux pas here, a faux pas there,
In this fashion world, it leads without care!

It mimics a parrot, squawking on high,
With colors so bright, it catches the eye.
A sudden sneeze, and it flutters away,
"Catch me if you can!" it seems to say!

The fabric is giggling, oh can't you tell?
With stories to share, it spins quite the spell.
Hold it tight, or it might just flee,
In the realm of chic, it's wild and free!

Secrets Stitched into Time

Once upon a time, it had a job,
A fashion advisor with flair to rob.
It whispered style tips, oh-so-sly,
"Cinch in that waist, and make them sigh!"

In a cupboard dark, it stayed for years,
Collecting dust bunnies and fashion fears.
But once unfurled, it couldn't contain,
The funky discoveries it had to explain!

With polka dots here and stripes over there,
It thrived on chaos, the ultimate dare!
"Try mismatching me!" it dared with a grin,
For oddball stylings, it would always win!

In patterns of laughter, it found its groove,
Every fold a secret, every twist to prove.
So if you dare share a wild dressing tale,
This lively fabric will help you prevail!

A Twisted Yarn of Truth

In a forest of fabric, where secrets loom,
A yarn once tangled in a closet's gloom.
With every twist, it spun a new fluff,
"Did you hear the news? Fashion can be tough!"

It ponders the purpose of stripes and spots,
"I'm fabulous, but look at their knots!"
A comedian wrapped 'round the throat,
In a playful debate with a fashion vote!

It whispers, "Oh, darling, I'm truly the best,
With stories and laughs, I'll outshine the rest!"
Twisted threads harbor a joke or two,
Fashion wisdom from faux pas crew!

So next time you wear me, don't just retreat,
Let's strut down the street, feel that beat!
For a laugh here and there keeps life in sway,
In the world of textiles, that's how we play!

A Tapestry of Untamed Thoughts

In the cupboard, a hidden sight,
A scarf that dances day and night.
It sways and giggles with flair,
Daring the socks to give it a scare.

Its patterns spin tales of mischief,
With puns and jokes that are quite stiff.
A twist here, a twirl there,
It's the comedian of the wear and tear!

Each fold hides a laugh, a tease,
Tickling the air like a soft breeze.
A yawn escapes from a nearby chair,
Even it can't help but stop and stare.

Fashioned in colors that clash,
It leaps into wardrobes with a splash.
"Oh darling, don't wear me today!"
Chortles the scarf, in a funny way.

Gentle Cradle of Secrets

A quirky wrap, so full of jest,
With each twist it makes, it feels blessed.
Hiding secrets beneath its sheen,
Of awkward moments, and places unseen.

It giggles when you toss it aside,
Remembers the times you tried to hide.
A warm embrace, or a ticklish prank,
It's the life of the party, never dank.

Softly it whispers, "Let's have some fun,"
With each knot, a new story's begun.
Caught in a tussle with your winter coat,
They laugh together, that's no remote!

It adorns your neck, like a sprightly bard,
Making you smile, even when hard.
"Remember," it says with a spin and a wave,
"I'm the giggle that helps you behave!"

Enfolded Whispers Beneath

A twist of fabric, a giggle in thread,
Hiding the things that should stay unsaid.
"It tickles your neck, but who would know?
I'm twice the comedian, twice the show!"

The cat thinks it's prey, with eyes that gleam,
A playful game, a chaotic dream.
"Oh silly feline, it's not for you,"
As it quakes in laughter, a bright hue.

In a drawer it plans its next big prank,
A waddle, a wiggle, a cheeky swank.
Caution the days you choose to wear,
For it thrives on chaos, not a care!

Each fold a secret, a tale to unfold,
Of mischief and giggles, a sight to behold.
So don it with glee, let the yarns take flight,
For within those layers, humor feels right!

Threads that Bind and Betray

In the closet lurks a light-hearted tease,
With every stitch, it aims to please.
"Wrap me around, let's go be wild,
I promise you'll laugh, just like a child!"

Its edges fray, but it takes no blame,
In the games of fashion, it's always the same.
"Oh come, dear friend, let's sashay and sway,
Life's too short, let's humor the gray!"

When unwound, tales of blunders arise,
Of spilled coffee and unexpected cries.
"Did you trip? No worries, I'll puff and puff,
With me by your side, you'll never look tough!"

In a realm where fabric meets fate,
This scarf plays the joker, never late.
So wear it with zest, don't feel betrayed,
For laughter's the thread that will never fade.

The Truce of Style and Substance

In a drawer, style met a sock,
Said, "I can dance, it's quite a shock!"
Substance replied, with a grin so wide,
"Just don't trip, or I'll have to hide!"

They twirled and collided, a chaotic spree,
One sought the limelight, the other felt glee.
A truce was declared, both laughed in delight,
"Let's dress up the world, we'll rock day and night!"

Shadows Between the Threads

Underneath the layers, a tale so bright,
A polka dot whispered, "I'm quite the sight!"
Stripes chimed in, with colors so bold,
"Together, my friend, we'll break the mold!"

In shadows they danced, with sass and cheer,
Chasing the sunlight, erasing all fear.
A patchwork of laughter, made heads turn,
"Let's spin this world, as it twists and burns!"

Unseen Bonds of Fabric

A button shared gossip, it laughed so loud,
"Did you see that shirt? It's lost in the crowd!"
Thread teased the seam, with a wink and a jig,
"Together we'll shine, let's bust out a gig!"

In stitches they bonded, no frays in sight,
They twirled and they flipped, oh what a sight!
A friendship of fabric, sweet snip and snug,
Beneath all the layers, there's warmth with a hug!

Woven Whispers in Twilight

In twilight's embrace, the laces did sway,
With whispers of secrets, they started to play.
"Did you hear the news? The bow's quite a hit!
But the sad little tie just sits in a pit!"

Laughter erupted, a fabric parade,
Tassels and fringes, all pieces displayed.
They danced in the dusk, under moon's soft gleam,
In woven delights, they lived out their dream!

Emblems of Untamed Whispers

A vibrant tale, unspooled wide,
With threads of laughter, some can't hide.
Each twist and fold, a joke to share,
It tickles your thoughts, a playful dare.

Worn like a cape, it flutters and sways,
Tickling the neck in curious ways.
A sneaky nibble, a cheeky sting,
As joyful secrets it dares to bring.

Colorful antics, a dance of flair,
It whispers softly, secrets to dare.
In a whimsical twist, it makes you grin,
Tangled in mirth, let the fun begin!

Whispers of cotton and vibrant blends,
Unraveling stories that never ends.
As laughter weaves through fabric bright,
In every fold, a ticklish delight.

Specters of Sable and Silk

In shadows where silken whispers dwell,
Dreams come alive, but only time will tell.
A ghostly glide around the room,
Leaving you giggling, dispelling gloom.

Sable notes chipper in the dark,
Tickling your senses like a lark.
Mysterious chuckles in each twirl,
Unveiling the secrets that twist and whirl.

Brought to life by laughter's breath,
Clothed in humor, defying death.
These fabrics play tricks, a sly little tease,
Softening moments, bringing you ease.

In a spectral waltz of cloth and cheer,
A playful spirit that's always near.
With every fold, a chuckle so spry,
These threads of humor will never die.

The Hidden Heartbeat of Textiles

Underneath layers, a pulse so bright,
A playful rhythm that feels just right.
Each stitch a heartbeat, an echo of fun,
Whispers of mischief, like rays of the sun.

In cozy corners, it revels with glee,
Making you chuckle at what you can't see.
A tickle of fabric that knows just how,
To bring silly smiles, oh, what a wow!

With every fray, a tale to unfold,
Rustling the silence, it's daring and bold.
A dance of fibers, a zany parade,
In the hidden beats, the joy won't fade.

From vibrant sashes to patterns astute,
Each pulse of fabric lends a sweet hoot.
As patterns cavort, laughter ignites,
In the fabric's heart, joy always delights.

Cascade of Colors in the Wind

A riot of colors that leap and dive,
Rustling through breezes, where dreams come alive.
With every flap, a merry frolic,
Transforming the air into something symbolic.

Swaying and swirling, a giggling affair,
The hues know the secrets, the jokes in the air.
They tickle the senses, a vibrant parade,
Making you chuckle, never dismayed.

Caught in a whirlwind, a fabric spree,
Like laughter unleashed, wild and free.
Every color a punchline, a twist of delight,
In this joyous tango, everything feels right.

As they tumble and dance, bright ribbons gleam,
Painting the day with a whimsical dream.
In this cascade, let your spirit soar,
For in every flutter, there's laughter galore.

An Enigma Wrapped in Threads

A twist and a turn, it starts to sing,
Wrapped in colors, it's quite the thing.
A dance of fabric, with secrets grand,
You won't believe what hides in hand!

A tug, a pull, what's this? A joke?
A knit mishap, or witty folk?
When laughter comes, it twists and twirls,
Unraveling stories of playful swirls!

In chilly weather, it plays so sly,
Warming hearts, while making them cry.
It whispers tales of times gone by,
While twirling around, just look and sigh!

So don't you dare stash it away,
For with every loop, it loves to play.
An enigma, in threads, full of cheer,
Let the laughter ring, the warmth draw near!

Silhouette of Secrets

A shadowy form, it flits and bops,
In colors so bright, it never stops.
Once in the closet, now on a spree,
With giggles and wiggles, it sets us free!

It pulls at my neck, a playful tease,
Whispers of mischief, carried by a breeze.
With each swish and sway, it brings delight,
A funny little fit for a quirky night.

Knots and loops, oh what a sight,
It tells the tales of silly fright.
With a wink and a curl, it starts to dance,
The perfect partner for a comical prance!

In shadows it hides, with a chuckle and grin,
A silly companion, let's let the fun begin!
Wear it with glee on this lively day,
For it holds the secrets that laugh and play!

The Gentle Pull of Hidden Stories

A tug on my neck, oh what's this?
Do I hear whispers? I can't resist!
With fibers of fun, it pulls me close,
Unraveling tales, like a playful ghost!

It wraps me up, snug as a hug,
Dancing through laughs, oh how it plugs!
With every loop, it shares a grin,
A charming companion, let the antics begin!

Twists and turns, it tickles my chin,
This fabric's a jokester, where to begin?
It whispers softly of all things bright,
In the cozy warmth of a starry night.

So here we go, let laughter soar,
With stories to tell, and smiles to store.
A gentle pull on this cheeky ride,
Let's celebrate this yarn, and enjoy the glide!

Knitted Memories of Softness

In the softest fibers, laughter's spun,
Twisting around like a roller run.
Knitted with care, and a dash of thrill,
Every stitch a giggle, an unspoken will!

It rolls off the shelf, with a playful chirp,
Under the sun, it starts to burp!
With memories woven, it gives a wink,
Proving that wool can even think!

Each loop a whisper, each twist a jest,
It drapes around us, hours of zest.
With every wear, it shares a grin,
In a world of warmth, where joy begins!

So wrap it up snug, and join the fun,
A tapestry of laughter, for everyone.
With knitted memories tucked in tight,
We'll weave new tales in sheer delight!

www.ingramcontent.com/pod-product-compliance
Lightning Source LLC
Chambersburg PA
CBHW060138230426
43661CB00003B/474